Eye Level

Jenny Morris

Leaf by Leaf is an imprint of Cinnamon Press.
www.cinnamonpress.com

The right of Jenny Morris to be identified as author of this work has been asserted by her in accordance with the Copyright, Designs and Patent Act, 1988. © 2023, Jenny Morris.

ISBN 978-1-78864-887-5

British Library Cataloguing in Publication Data. A CIP record for this book can be obtained from the British Library.

Designed and typeset in Bodoni by Cinnamon Press. Cover design by Adam Craig

Cinnamon Press is represented by Inpress Ltd.

Acknowledgements

'Jerm' and 'Joj' were published in *Urban Space*
'The Best Good in the World' was published in *Pennine Platform*
'Bellchildren' was published in *Cracking-On*

About the Author

Jenny Morris writes poetry and fiction. Her work has been widely published. After living in many different places in UK and abroad, she settled in Norfolk. Her previous collections are *Urban Space, The Sin Eater, Lunatic Moon, Somnambulist* and *Domestic Damage*, published by Cinnamon Press. Her pamphlet *Keeping Secrets* won the Cinnamon Press pamphlet prize. Her novel, *Borderline*, is also published by Cinnamon Press.

Contents

for all my family

Eye Level

TAKEN FROM LIFE

From sirens and shelters,
smocking and rationing,
and snaps of a stranger who
returned as a father.

From eye problems, girdle scones,
oat cakes, parkin and smokies,
millstone grit, gumption
and swings chained on Sundays.

From jute and jet, north and west,
coasts and moors, lost music,
dance, and an obsession
with the 'Freak Fat Lady' at the Fair.

From liberty bodices,
Fair Isle jumpers, anxieties and bad
dreams, always understanding
the necessity of smiling.

From self-reinvention, literal
cities and the metaphorical dark
forest, from wrong choices and
culs-de-sac.

BECOME LIKE A BOTTLE IN THE SMOKE

They grin like a dog, and run about through the city.
She was asked
to help with lying-in,
with laying-out the dead,
to give poultices, pull teeth,
break up fights,
care for children.
She told her bees
when her husband
and son died.

Whose feet they hurt in the stocks:
the iron entered into his soul.
Her cabinet was stocked
with wych hazel
and herbal remedies.
Her kitchen was scented
with beef tea, boiled onions,
pickled pears and lavender.
She knitted woollen stockings
on four needles, could turn a heel
while advising on chilblains and poisons.

Scant measure is abominable.
She began the day with a glass
of hot water and a slice of lemon.
The feather bed aired,
rugs beaten, vegetables dug,
yeast bought, bread baked,
neighbours helped, letters written.
When the work ended
her stone hot water bottle
was filled late at night.

The mountains skipped like rams:
and the little hills like young sheep.
She wore a blouse dyed with tea,
her father's heavy gold watch chain
when she poured, Wine that makes glad
the heart of man. Since her twenties
her hair was white.
Her name was Lavinia.
She was known as 'Love'.

MAKESHIFT

Your new eyes opened on a boy's
round head in an elm, a room
full of books, an old woman
with a stick and a trilby hat,
a ship rigged in a Dimple Haig bottle.
Your mother cooked *sans* eggs,
butter, sugar or meat.

You wore knee socks, kilt, ballet slippers.
Your scratched satchel was called Billy
Mundy. Identity was just a name
on a gabardine. A hand me down.
You came from whalers and baleen
where trains bewailed the night.
You collected angel scraps.

Your concrete air-raid shelter
pebble-dashed itself with
stuck-together pairs of snails.
Curious, you pulled them apart.
All games were perplexing.
The Brick Ponds' girl said, *You
spoil everybody's pleasure.*

NETTA

Like a stick of rock, her name
Netta went all through. This
was the Edinburgh variety—dry
and crumbling pastel chalk—while
she was sturdy, solid, unbroken
in catastrophes.

She used her tartan rug for garden
picnics, with deckchairs, cut glass jars
of rhubarb jam and lace napkins
in horn rings. She liked mealie puddings,
potted haugh, potato cakes, Scotch broth
with pearl barley and cabbage hearts.

In Angus she left early
for the two hour journey to work
wearing her dark hat, black coat
with a Cairngorm brooch.
Her bag held umbrella, a paper
poke of boilings and one of tablet.

She was outspoken, in command,
liked order, high standards.
Her life was service and drudgery.
In old age she missed the jute ship
foghorns, lights of passing steam
trains. You shared her medicines.

WHERE'S HOME?

Dreaming, wanting to go home,
you can't remember the address.
Anxious, awaking, you're an infant
again at your grandmother's house.
She was from cattle-dealers. As a girl
had to help pole-axe cows, unwillingly.

It was easy to burrow into her
all-encompassing heart. There,
with her, the best place was the pale
attic with its feather bed and skylight.
The worst was a grim and mouldy
outbuilding called 'the rat house'.

In a cupboard was a smaller house, a toy
butcher's shop with striped awning.
You took it out by the flower-filled trough
to play with on the smooth flag-stones.
The joints of meat and sausage strings,
pink, red and white, hung on tiny hooks.

You cast yourself in all roles: shopkeeper
and customers. You murmur all morning.
Hungry, You taste the wares. Baffling
hard plaster with a taste of dust.

AT THE TOP OF THE HILL

Shuffling sheep behind these dry-stone walls
watch lambs that skitter on the tussocked fields.
This nursery's run-down, greenhouses bare.
Your father spends his weekends toiling here.
Your brother's busy climbing blossoming trees
above the scratching of the pecking hens.
The baby, pram-bound, by a washing line
is mesmerised by fluttering slips and sheets.

A child with plaits, in dungarees and boots,
you prance, a turned-out dancer, all along
the edges of the open garden frames
avoiding tender plants and broken glass.
You are Pavlova, sometimes you're Fonteyn.
Your conjured tutu shimmers with each leap.
All thrushes drumming snails to death on stones
must be passed by as you just pirouette
for shadow watchers in the flower beds.

You spin off into spaces of your own.
And far below you stretches all the world
in jigsaw shapes of scattered green and grey,
of empty, winding roads, the way ahead.

ON THE HIGH PENNINES

Creaking springs, glossy quilt.
Utility bed where you are stuck fast.
Cold lino, rumpled mat, wind-rattled window.
Ice inside in February. Matching glass
figures frozen on the bookcase.

Outside, metal-tipped clogs clatter
downhill. Miners to their early shift.
Guttural sheep and dogs rail at their passing.

From your bed, through the window
you see only sky, fast-flying clouds, dark birds.
Far below, you know that the hills and dales
stretch out, marked by drystone walls,
stunted trees and soot-blackened slabs
of houses with weavers' windows.
Steel grey smoke signals city mills.

You are young, ill, book-reliant, irrational,
not fearing the great bazaar ahead.
Seeing the sun dissolve, the wind weep,
rain quiver, forces a pencil into your hand.

YOUNG TRIOLETS

Those words are so painful,
Get lost. Let me go.
Their meaning is baneful.
Those words are so painful.
They sound so disdainful
your ego can't grow.
Those words are so painful,
Get lost. Let me go.

Great Scott! You are falling
in love once again.
It's really appalling
that you can't help falling.
You just feel like bawling
for fear of the pain.
Great Scott, you are falling
for him once again.

PRESENTS

He stood on your doorstep
with a gift,
a coypu he'd just shot.
It hung from his hand
with its blood-matted fur,
eyes dark in its wet head.
You thought, *This youth
doesn't know me at all.*

You developed a gift
for choosing men
unsuitable for you.
So you learned the art
of silence, of creating
offerings: pourboire,
cumshaw, baksheesh,
favours, smiles.

You remembered sitting
on an Arbroath sea wall,
learning about monks
from your father. Kindness
like the sun, coloured
the abbey stones rose.

ILLUSTRATING THE PAST

You knew desire the night you heard his voice.
A tone so deep, designed to dominate,
so mesmerising that you had no choice
but listen, touch your tangled hair and wait.
Seduced at once by his hard-burning eyes
you followed where he led because you sensed
to be with him would be some paradise.
He seemed so worldly-wise, experienced,
most tall and dark and confident of men.
What he could see in you they never knew
but you recall each vivid moment then,
the passion of your every rendezvous.
Depict your past as an Assyrian frieze—
he's out in front eclipsing all with ease.

CITY OF LIGHT

This is a city of monuments
boulevards and streets
named after great dead men.
Under chestnut trees
where birds sing in French
elegant girls leave traces
of scent in their wake.

Men call *Ça va?*
and, mocking, *et alors?*
as they swing their thin hips
past patchy sycamore bark
and the slow moving
silver river.

Below ancient stone gargoyles
and mutilated saints
garçons in long white aprons
carry cognac and croissants
to the melody of 'La Vie en Rose'
for Parisians who look
with the eyes of love.

But you in a home-sewn
shift dress, approaching
la Place de la Concorde
hear tumbrels on the cobbles
and see women knitting
by that guillotine
lit by an early
and tarnished moon.

WHEN

When they were born they tore out half your heart.
You never knew sensations strong as these.

When they were born you learned what love could do.
The sum of it filled seas and skies, lit stars.

When they were born all other creatures here
lost force, and faded, dwindled to the edge.

When they were born all dangers fell like rain.
You heard the thunder, watched with different eyes.

Now they are grown and you are self-absorbed
but know you'll feel forever incomplete.

CITY OF SCARS

Above the Iron Curtain
a plane dropped through clouds,
roared, stalled, crept into Tempelhof,
uneasy space between buildings.

Bomb-rubble Teufelsberg,
pocked blocks, ruins, bones
formed the haunted capital
peopled by masks.

They worked in secret rooms.
Understood codes. Listened.
Shivered into the darkness.
Divided city. Steel wall. Cold War.

There Brandenburger Tor reared,
last frontier of the west. Frost
wires trailed across the sky. Men
laboured in tunnels. Ice bit deep.

Chill drumbeats, echoes of marching feet
slammed the streets. Tanks rolled.
Different uniforms came and went.
Disturbing howl and pound of wreckers,

mechanical hammers, diggers,
machines levelling, rattle
of lifts and scaffolding.
So the towers fell and rose.

On the Kurfurstendamm, Hilke
and Margarethe crammed cream cakes.
Hotel Kempinski filled with furs.
Checkpoint Charlie froze solid.

East of the wall, watch-tower soldiers
aimed along the death strip. Imagine
Kathe in her trembling cellar waiting
for the Red Army. Hess in Spandau.

Always, above, black hooded crows cried
flew from east to west and back again
unhindered by orders.

BERLIN CITYSCAPE

You're not a camera, more a word sharpshooter
behind curtains here on the ninth floor
of a rented flat in Reichsstrasse
in a haze of strangers' dust and wood polish,
blaming the flawed post-war window glass
for the ripples in your vision which may,
of course, be caused by tears.
Tasting metal, you focus down
on little views of people's lives.

Evening, and the lights come on, rectangular eyes
glinting from the dark cliff-faces that enclose
this concrete courtyard. Lit targets,
tiny stage sets where midgets
betray their lives in your sights.
Glimpsed glances. Blink and they're gone
in the flick of a switch. There's
a credible dungeon scene, grimmig und garstig.
Blackness cuts stories before they're ended.

Morning, and you note a wall's sad graffito:
Herr Hackfleisch, ich kann doch nicht hexen.
A false-nosed old woman tends her plants
oils glossy emerald leaves, waters pots daily.
Her carried coffin lurches over cobbles through
the archway. Living greenery droops in her window.
High above, underwear and stained knitted garments
from unseen babies flap from a balcony. Wails echo
across the chasm. A caged bird hangs in a casement.

Yellow, frantic, it flutters against visible hands.
Music spills through the air—nostalgic, discordant.
Raucous televisions flicker, roar and undermine.
Men call out, swear, make impossible demands.
Shrill hidden women respond. Hot odours
of spoiled blutwurst and cabbage rise to the drainpipes.
Sulky lovers slap and tangle on sofas. Children run
with broken aeroplanes. A lost dog whines.
Watching, you pin them down with damaged words.

JERM

This solemn, solid three-year-old person
is a master of the penetrating stare.
Like a compact blue-eyed owl
he subjects the world to his unblinking scrutiny.
Ruffled blond hair *en brosse*,
stout old lederhosen his dirt armour.
With wrong-footed boots
he roosts on the wall,
waiting for the dustbin lorry—
highlight of his week.
He's conversational, full of reasonable questions:
But why is it so?
and *What's this, please?*
Always solicitous of insects
though unsure of spiders,
interested in cake,
boilers, active machines,
wheels that go round.
A sitter-under tables and chairs,
pretend driver, director of operations:
always thoughtful;
part of us.
He shows us first
the meaning of real pride.

NASSIM ROAD

An old colonial house
decays
its walls covered
with leprous mould
bedded in with palms
and hibiscus.
Heat hangs
chickens scratch
round a pile of papaya.
The owner sits
on his verandah. His belly
bulges under
his sweat-stained vest.
Beside him
his Chinese girl
plays with their babies
on the steps.
No-one will ever know
what she thinks.
Paint flakes
from pillars
shutters hang crooked
ceiling fans lurch.
Stone floors are cool
under bare feet.
There are no locks
on doors.
Someone cries
in a distant room.

JOJ

Grey hands I loved beside the ballet barre,
small, lined and scratchy hands
of little Joj.
A high-instepped, curly-toed girl,
determined, in a dusty leotard
repeating pliés, battements, pirouettes,
as naturally as breathing,
She danced the years away
always in time
being her own metronome.

Later those heavy-duty fingers
buffeted the old piano
as she sang the blues, fast jazz
or secretly lyrical for grandmother Maggot
Pale Hands I Loved Beside the Shalimar.

She dragged that painted didgeridoo
across the world
for deep andante whiffling and rumbling,
Always dressed in mellifluous black,
black, black or purple.
Her laughter always clangorous.

On two furious speeding wheels,
in masculine, inviolable leathers
she was menacing,
At filling-stations, her helmet off,
hair flowing down, she could blush
and men stopped cursing.

A tall Juno, she strode the streets
like a proud figurehead
with clear carved bones,
short upper lip and deepset coal-blue eyes
that searched for the horizon,
listening for a stepping-out beat.
She followed to improvise
the strange music
of cathedrals, choirs, machines,
spoons and saws.

Everything is melody to her.

EYE LEVEL

Your eyes are too small
and too close together,
the optician's assistant
says, so are unsuitable
for the elegant
frames you've chosen.
You ignore this advice
from the girl with fat
ankles like
doughnut socks.

Back home, you enlarge
your pin-prick eyes
with black lines
mascara, glitter
and false eyelashes.
Your wrap-around shades
are a last resort.

You've made eyes
at men lots of times.
And at him and him.
You've been making
a spectacle of yourself
for years.

TEARS SHED AND UNSHED

As a child you remained dry-eyed
for rabbit and dog deaths.
The demise of any Little Nell
left you unmoved.
Over years you walked away from
shouters and beaters.

In the Interrogation Wing you learned
that true weeping played no part
in the scheme of instruction.
You earned intimidation money.
It was just a test. Men weakened
by a girl's sobs were no use.

Tears became devalued
rolling on tap like moonstones.
Cry for physical pain, a wound,
you thought. Pour salt in it
for healing. Being shouted at
by bad-tempered men
in uniform was not much
of a change.

AN AMERICAN IN ALDERSHOT

He came up in his 1980 Oldsmobile
fresh from Pennsylvania,
muscled, tanned forearm resting
on the left-hand wound-down window.

Going my way? he asked.
You climbed in to the scent
of unfamiliar cologne.

He drove fast, circled the roundabout
the wrong way. Startled drivers
in oncoming cars mouthed,
swerved away from you.

He laughed, *I sure won't do that again.*
Glen Campbell's 'Southern Nights'
pumped inside, then the blare
of Blondie's 'Call Me'
made your heart thump in time.

On cruise control to Greenham Common
where women outside the missile silos
put white blooms in the base fence.
A scent of honeysuckle and birdsong
rising to the bluest English sky.

Bottles of Jim Beam clinked in the trunk.
Your man's dollars stacked in his Levi's
back pocket. Your children's letters
warm and worn in your bag.

VOLUSIA COUNTY

A fish crow coughs from the top
of Ponce de Leon Towers and drops
to scavenge and rattle in the trash can
beside you where shells like human ears
poke up through the white sand
and the ocean can hiss and wheeze.
From inland comes the mournful
hoot of a monster freight train.
The county was smashed by hurricanes
but feather duster palms re-sprout
and new seawalls rise by roofs
still shielded by tarpaulins.

Passing clouds cross their plump
fingers as grandmas, Mah jong players
with men's haircuts, cruise the Dixie
Freeway in their Cadillacs and Chevrolets
past Kitty Care and Gun Shop and Sod
the Nursery to the Plazas to down
their beers and boatsinker pies.
Pelicans from the Indian River
tanglewood float in the hot air.
Lines of odd numbers today.
Your fortune cookie reads, *You
have a quiet and unobtrusive nature.*

SHORE MUSIC

Left, right, left, right.
His boots are blows along the front.
For years he marched in uniform
in troops, in squads, in distant wars.
Today, unchanged, he must keep time
to this, the beat of his sure heart.
Arms swinging, straight-backed, he can't break
his measured rhythm. No mistake.

Here on this strand's an orchestra:
percussion of bootbeat tattoo,
the shingle sounds its loud drumrolls,
ships hoot far off while gulls cry out,
the water sighs, surf rises, falls,
waves crash and rush in endless sea.
Their echoes make a symphony.

It's early. Stars pale among clouds.
A yellow glow, a hollow moon,
until a weak and wintry sun
rolls up from under this sea's rim.
Advancing and returning, he
retains his pace, although he hears
the standard bearers' even tread.
Time's captive. His own hourglass
can't break yet in the sharp salt scent.
The falling sand is still unspent.

DECORATION

On certain family occasions she wore
pinned to her dress, the Australian gift:
a spray of white emu feathers. You saw

how often for comfort she gave it swift
touches. Others could hurl themselves downstairs.
Not her, yet, aware she was adrift

in the wrong life. An infant, scared
and unarmed, she'd been sent off deprived
of parents. In muddled age she liked to wear

what she called her 'kangaroo feathers'. Contrived
to flaunt this crest, this hackle-medal, wherever
she was, to show that she survived.

She knew that in a different place altogether
kangaroos grow perfect feathers.

LAND LIFE

The old grey widow-maker lodged
inside his head. For all his life
as plants must turn towards the light
he had a wish to go to sea,
but spent his days behind a desk
without salt air or sea birds' cries.
When young, he saved and bought a ship
fine-drawn inside a whisky flask.

In northern ports he saw the old
tea clippers, schooners, battleships.
Escaped by steamships off to find
the Viking longboats, whalers, brigs
and barques which sailed the Baltic Sea.

In youth sometimes in gale force winds
he sat alone on deck to eat
the bacon left by shipmates sick
in galleys down below. At war,
in convoys, sailed round Africa
through oceans, Red Sea to the Med.
He wrote, not of the floating mines,
torpedo onslaughts, but of gleams
of light on water, flying fish,
of sharks and one lone albatross.

When he was old and crippled
in his land-locked room, he liked to read
of famous voyages. He saw
cloud traffic fuse and wane, he rode
the battling waves to distant lands,
at nightfall anchored at dream piers
and on his watch the fleet moved on.
He viewed his own ship there, encased
in glass, becoming larger as
he dwindled down inside his bones,
until he reached another shore.

THE BEST GOOD IN THE WORLD

Outside the chapel you all stand
like dummies in your black finery,
your unaccustomed, pinching shoes,
your tight white collars, your jet
jewellery, your decent hats,
your decent expressions, dark
like the heavy-lidded sky,
while an expected cold wind
blows leaves over your feet.
Today the gold fire of sun
has burned away to ash.

You stand in varying degrees
of pain. Pale-faced, sleepless
mourners next to pall-bearers
where scented white flowers
are lamps in the shadows,
silent lily trumpets drawing
attention to the one who is absent.

Now you learn that a hard look
can be called heartbreak.
Your father's saying sounds in your head.
She was a good. The last word
not an adjective, but a noun.
Your parents were both that. They
gave you what you all are, at this time.
Your varying degrees of good.

BELLCHILDREN

Lavinia spoke. *They warm my heart,*
these children from my flesh and blood.
That rang a bell. Your mother said,
I'll never rear her. But she did.
She lost her mother early on,
went searching for her ever since.
A ruined life's a sad affair.
Your flawed old heart is knocking on.
It needs the glow of filial care.
Just like a clock it marks the hours
while counting down and wearing out,
as church bells ring to ward off storms,
extinguish fires, spin devils off.
You hear the chimes which drive the beat
as echoes of what's gone before.
While on the grass these children play,
they laugh and call and sing in time.
Such small inspectors claiming love.
Facsimiles in miniature,
the clear-eyed gaze of long ago.
You're past. They're present, future years.
The story must go on and on.
As weeks roll by, it helps to know
these infants' ways take cadence from
this rocking cradle of your heart.

YOU REMEMBER

You begin to live
in a foreign language
where memories rattle.

Hunched pines lament
with you on a sea cliff
until the howl of a gale
scatters your words.

Wind blows over empty land,
hollow reeds bend,
trains cry in the night
and lanterns burn late.

Your throat aches.
Your thoughts, like the air
spin out of control. You
are someone else entirely.

As rooks fly home
the evening fades in blankness.
You forget. You forget.

SING, SING

As a night fish in a net
with eyes of frozen glass
you long for him.

The moon's silvers burn cold.
The bronze face of the sun
roars and brands. The strap
of the wind wounds.
Firewater breaks him.
You are the sound
of ripped silk.

In your house alabaster birds
sleep. There are bees
inside your hollow head.

Now there is no-one to take
your hand, that of a lost child.
You are alone, unwrapped
to the bone, and must clean
out your heart.
The gaunt dead are yours.
You must talk to them.
The stars sing to you in the dark.

TERRA INCOGNITA

The days of your life are few.
You breathe in a lily scent
while wandering winds may rise
and fall, bringing the taste of salt
or ashes, scent of smoke:
memory stains your bones.

Those whom you loved are lost.
Their shadows reach out to you,
they whisper in silver birches,
they sigh in the crumpled roses,
their eyes are like tiny lamps,
the slow wheeling stars in space.

You'll talk in a haunted speech
dance in the dark of night
death will arrive for you.
You'll notice his little face
high up in the window there
as you are approaching home.